MICHAEL THOMAS

NFL STAR

By Douglas Lynne

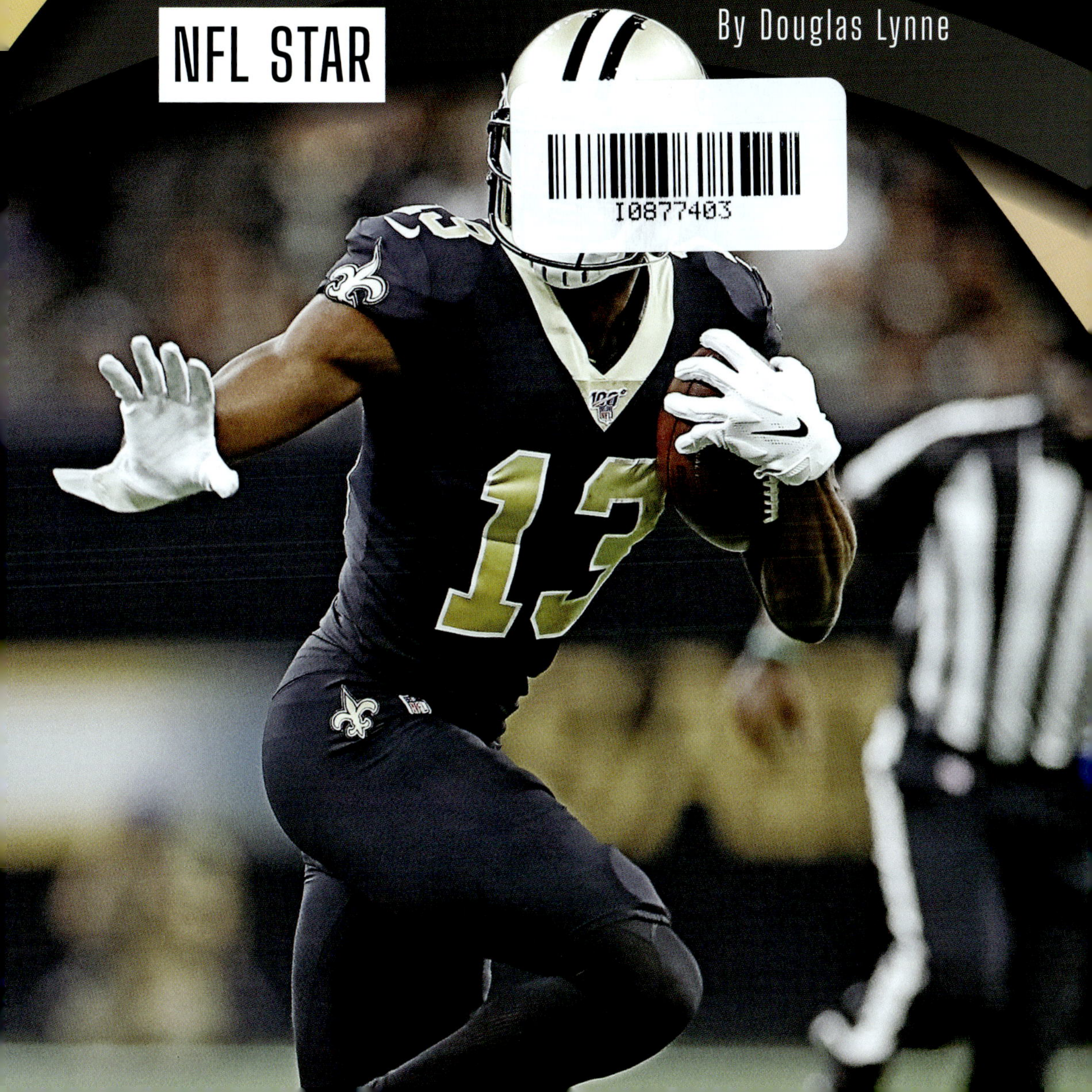

Book design by Jake Nordby
Cover design by Jake Slavik

Photographs ©: Greg Trott/AP Images, cover, 1; Bill Feig/AP Images, 4, 8–9, 19, 23; G. Newman Lowrance/AP Images, 6; Chris Bernacchi/AP Images, 10; Rick Scuteri/AP Images, 12; Perry Knotts/AP Images, 15; Tony Avelar/AP Images, 16; Shutterstock Images, 20; Red Line Editorial, 22

Press Box Books, an imprint of Press Room Editions.

Library of Congress Control Number: 2020901602

ISBN
978-1-63494-223-2 (library bound)
978-1-63494-241-6 (paperback)
978-1-63494-259-1 (epub)
978-1-63494-277-5 (hosted ebook)

Distributed by North Star Editions, Inc.
2297 Waters Drive
Mendota Heights, MN 55120
www.northstareditions.com

Printed in the United States of America
082020

ABOUT THE AUTHOR

Douglas Lynne is a freelance writer. He spent many years working in the media, first in newspapers and later for online organizations, covering everything from breaking news to politics to entertainment to sports. He lives in Minneapolis, Minnesota.

TABLE OF CONTENTS

13

1

CAN'T GUARD MIKE

The New Orleans Saints and the Los Angeles Rams gathered at the line of scrimmage. Just four minutes remained in the fourth quarter of their 2018 game. The Saints led 38–35, and now they were driving again.

Quarterback Drew Brees dropped back into the pocket. He looked downfield. Michael Thomas, his best wide receiver, was open. Brees pumped the ball once

Michael Thomas coasts into the end zone against the Rams.

Thomas torched the Rams with 12 catches for 211 yards that day.

and threw a long pass. The ball spiraled through the air.

Thomas reached his hands out. He caught the ball and tucked it close to his side. Thomas nearly stumbled just past midfield. Rams players raced to catch up. But Thomas gained his footing and sped downfield.

No one was near him now. The hometown crowd at the Superdome cheered louder and louder. Thomas breezed into the end zone for a 72-yard touchdown. His catch sealed the game for the Saints. They won 45–35.

Thomas has proven over and over he is one of the best receivers in the

PLAYING THROUGH PAIN

Thomas left the last game of the 2019 regular season with a wrapped hand. He took it easy in the next two weeks of practice. But he played in the wild-card playoff game against the Minnesota Vikings. He caught seven passes for 70 yards. Thomas later revealed his hand was broken.

Thomas greets Saints fans after the big win over the Rams.

National Football League (NFL). Rarely had he been better than in this game against the Rams. His 211 receiving yards was a career high and helped the Saints win an important game.

Upon entering the league in 2016, Thomas improved every year. In 2019, he signed a contract extension for $100 million. He became the highest-paid wide receiver in the NFL. But Thomas is not resting. He has big plans for the future.

B1G
83

2
BECOMING A STAR

Michael Thomas was born on March 3, 1993, in Los Angeles, California. Michael was surrounded by football from a young age. His uncle is Keyshawn Johnson. Johnson was one of the best wide receivers in the NFL. He played for 11 seasons.

When Michael was only three years old, his dad brought him to Johnson's football practices. Michael ran along the

Michael learned a lot about football from being around the game as a kid.

Michael demonstrated his strong grip as he climbed to higher levels of football.

sidelines. He loved watching the players put in their work to improve their skills.

Michael liked to play football. He joined his high school team as a junior. Michael was tall. That is good for a wide receiver. But he was not very strong. He did not get much playing time.

Michael wanted to improve his strength. He and his father made a plan. They set up a gym in the garage. Michael worked hard to become stronger during the summer between his junior and senior years.

STRONG HANDS

In high school, Michael focused on strengthening his grip. Some of his classmates thought it was strange. But Michael knew his hard work would pay off. Having a strong grip helps him make big catches when it matters most.

His hard work paid off. That fall, Michael became the go-to receiver for his team. He was ready to play college football.

Ohio State University's coaching staff liked what they saw in Michael. They offered him a football scholarship. He believed he was ready to play as a freshman. But he made a lot of mistakes. Coaches told him he was not mature enough. The next year, Michael sat out the whole season as a redshirt.

Michael knew he had to make some big changes. When he came back the next year, his coaches saw a lot of improvement. They knew he was ready to play. Michael spent two more seasons at Ohio State. Then he left for the NFL.

The New Orleans Saints chose him in the second round of the 2016 NFL Draft. Michael was going to play professional football.

MICHAEL THOMAS
OHIO STATE CAREER STATISTICS

- **2012** - 3 catches, 22 yards
- **2014** - 54 catches, 799 yards, 9 touchdowns
- **2015** - 56 catches, 781 yards, 9 touchdowns

Michael displayed his skills for NFL teams during workouts before the 2016 draft.

3

LEAGUE LEADER

During his rookie season of 2016, Thomas set himself apart from the crowd. He caught 92 passes for 1,137 yards. Quarterback Drew Brees often relied on Thomas during important plays. But that was not enough for Thomas. He wanted to keep improving his game.

In the next three years, Thomas made history. He became only the fifth player in

Thomas quickly became a go-to receiver for quarterback Drew Brees (9).

NFL history ever to catch more than 100 passes for 1,000 yards three years in a row.

Thomas set records again and again early in his career. In his first three seasons, he caught 321 passes. No other player had more receptions in their first three seasons.

Thomas caught 149 passes during the 2019 regular season. That was an NFL record. Thomas's receptions totaled 1,725 yards. That broke his own team record. He had set it a year earlier with 1,405 receiving yards.

Thomas ended the 2019 season by being selected to the Pro Bowl. It marked his third selection in three seasons. He also helped the Saints reach the playoffs all three seasons. But each year ended in heartbreak. The Saints were knocked out by the Minnesota Vikings in close games in the 2017 and 2019 playoffs.

Thomas makes an acrobatic touchdown catch against the Eagles in the 2018 playoffs.

Thomas represented the Saints in the Pro Bowl in January 2020.

The 2018 playoffs were even more painful for Thomas and the Saints. In the first round, they beat the Philadelphia Eagles 20–14. Thomas was dominant. He caught 12 passes for 171 yards and scored the go-ahead touchdown. But the next week, with a trip to the Super Bowl on the line, New Orleans lost at home in overtime to the Rams.

DOING IT FOR THE KIDS

Thomas is a leader for his team. But he is also a leader off the field. In December 2019, he visited a children's hospital to hand out gifts to the patients. For some of the kids, a chance to meet one of their heroes was the biggest gift of all.

Michael Thomas continued to improve his strength and quickness. He's already become one of the top wide receivers in the NFL. Next, he wants to help the Saints win a Super Bowl. With his love of hard work, he's shown that anything is possible.

TIMELINE MAP

1. **Los Angeles, California: 1993**
   Michael Thomas is born on March 3.
2. **Columbus, Ohio: 2012**
   Thomas begins his college football career at Ohio State.
3. **Chicago, Illinois: 2016**
   The New Orleans Saints select Thomas with a second-round pick in the NFL Draft.
4. **Orlando, Florida: 2018**
   Thomas plays in his first Pro Bowl on January 28.
5. **New Orleans, Louisiana: 2018**
   Thomas catches 12 passes for a career-high 211 yards against the Rams on November 4.
6. **New Orleans, Louisiana: 2019**
   Thomas signs a contract extension with the Saints for $100 million.
7. **Charlotte, North Carolina: 2019**
   Thomas ends the regular season with an NFL-record 149 catches as the Saints beat the Carolina Panthers.

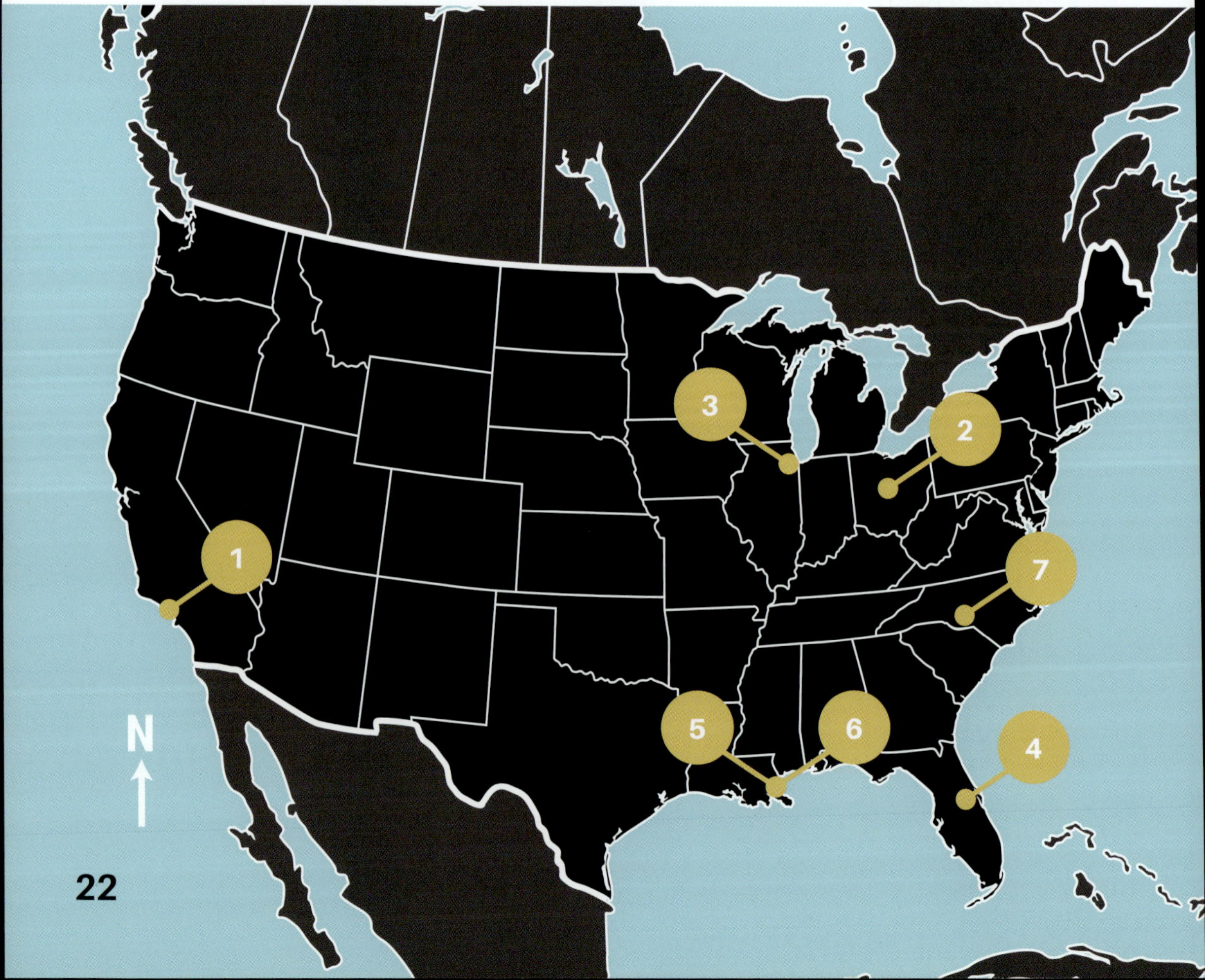

AT-A-GLANCE

MICHAEL THOMAS

Birth date: March 3, 1993

Birthplace: Los Angeles, California

Position: Wide receiver

Height: 6 feet 3 inches

Weight: 212 pounds

Current team: New Orleans Saints (2016–)

Past team: Ohio State Buckeyes (2012–15)

Major awards: NFL Offensive Player of the Year (2019), NFC Offensive Player of the Month (November 2019), First Team All-Pro (2018, 2019), Pro Bowl (2017, 2018, 2019), NFL All-Rookie Team (2016)

Accurate through the 2019 season.

MORE INFORMATION

To learn more about Michael Thomas, go to **pressboxbooks.com/AllAccess**.

These links are routinely monitored and updated to provide the most current information available.

GLOSSARY

dominant
In charge or in command of a situation.

draft
A system by which sports leagues divide up new talent.

extension
An agreement to lengthen a contract.

line of scrimmage
The place on the field where a play starts.

redshirt
A college athlete who practices but doesn't play in games to save a season of eligibility.

rookie
A first-year player.

scholarship
Money given to a student to cover college expenses, often in exchange for playing sports.

INDEX